2020 SUPPLEMENT TO
CONSTITUTIONAL LAW
CASES, COMMENTS, AND QUESTIONS

Thirteenth Edition

■ ■ ■

Jesse H. Choper
Earl Warren Professor of Public Law (Emeritus)
University of California, Berkeley

Michael C. Dorf
Robert S. Stevens Professor of Law
Cornell University

Richard H. Fallon, Jr.
Story Professor of Law
Harvard University

Frederick Schauer
David and Mary Harrison Distinguished Professor of Law
University of Virginia

AMERICAN CASEBOOK SERIES®

WEST ACADEMIC PUBLISHING

American Casebook Series is a trademark registered in the U.S. Patent and Trademark Office.

© 2020 LEG, Inc. d/b/a West Academic
    444 Cedar Street, Suite 700
    St. Paul, MN 55101
    1-877-888-1330

West, West Academic Publishing, and West Academic are trademarks of West Publishing Corporation, used under license.

Printed in the United States of America

ISBN: 978-1-68467-986-7

PREFACE

In ordinary years, the Court releases all of its opinions by the end of June. However, due to public health concerns, in the most recent Term the Court postponed a number of oral arguments, which in turn delayed the release of opinions in some cases. This Supplement is up to date through cases decided by July 6, 2020. However, in order to ensure timely distribution, we were unable to include cases decided after that date. Four cases decided by the Court on the last two days of the Term would have been included in this volume but came too late. Readers will be able to find material relating to them free of further charge on this title's product page at faculty.westacademic.com.

TABLE OF CONTENTS

TABLE OF CASES

The principal cases are in bold type.

2020 SUPPLEMENT TO
CONSTITUTIONAL LAW
CASES, COMMENTS, AND QUESTIONS

Thirteenth Edition

CHAPTER 1

NATURE AND SCOPE OF JUDICIAL REVIEW

■ ■ ■

2. POLITICAL QUESTIONS

P. 41, after *Nixon v. United States*:

RUCHO V. COMMON CAUSE
___ U.S. ___, 139 S.Ct. 2484, 204 L.Ed.2d 931 (2019).

CHIEF JUSTICE ROBERTS delivered the opinion of the Court.

Voters and other plaintiffs in North Carolina and Maryland challenged their States' congressional districting maps as unconstitutional partisan gerrymanders. The North Carolina plaintiffs complained that the State's districting plan discriminated against Democrats; the Maryland plaintiffs complained that their State's plan discriminated against Republicans. The plaintiffs alleged that the gerrymandering violated the First Amendment, the Equal Protection Clause of the Fourteenth Amendment, the Elections Clause, and Article I, § 2, of the Constitution.

[All agree that the partisan gerrymanders at issue in the two cases were deliberate and at least initially highly effective. In *Rucho*, the North Carolina case] one of the two Republicans chairing the redistricting committee [explained] that the map was drawn with the aim of electing ten Republicans and three Democrats because he did "not believe it [would be] possible to draw a map with 11 Republicans and 2 Democrats." One Democratic state senator objected that entrenching the 10–3 advantage for Republicans was not "fair, reasonable, [or] balanced" because, as recently as 2012, "Democratic congressional candidates had received more votes on a statewide basis than Republican candidates." [In] November 2016, North Carolina conducted congressional elections using the 2016 Plan [at issue in the litigation], and Republican candidates won 10 of the 13 congressional districts.

[The] second case before us is *Lamone v. Benisek*. In 2011, the Maryland Legislature—dominated by Democrats—undertook to redraw the lines of that State's eight congressional districts. The Governor at the time, Democrat Martin O'Malley, [appointed] a redistricting committee to help redraw the map. [The] Governor later testified that his aim was to "use the redistricting process to change the overall composition of

Maryland's congressional delegation to 7 Democrats and 1 Republican by flipping" one district. [The] 2011 Plan accomplished that by moving roughly 360,000 voters out of the Sixth District and moving 350,000 new voters in. Overall, the Plan reduced the number of registered Republicans in the Sixth District by about 66,000 and increased the number of registered Democrats by about 24,000. The map was adopted by a party-line vote. It was used in the 2012 election and succeeded in flipping the Sixth District. A Democrat has held the seat ever since.

[In] these cases we are asked to decide an important question of constitutional law. "But before we do so, we must find that the question is presented in a 'case' or 'controversy' that is, in James Madison's words, 'of a Judiciary Nature.'" *DaimlerChrysler Corp. v. Cuno*, 547 U. S. 332, 342 (2006) (quoting 2 Records of the Federal Convention of 1787, p. 430 (M. Farrand ed. 1966)). [The] question here is whether there is an "appropriate role for the Federal Judiciary" in remedying the problem of partisan gerrymandering—whether such claims are claims of *legal* right, resolvable according to *legal* principles, or political questions that must find their resolution elsewhere.

Partisan gerrymandering is nothing new. Nor is frustration with it. [The] Framers addressed the election of Representatives to Congress in the Elections Clause. Art. I, § 4, cl. 1. That provision assigns to state legislatures the power to prescribe the "Times, Places and Manner of holding Elections" for Members of Congress, while giving Congress the power to "make or alter" any such regulations. [The Court here cited historical examples of congressional regulation before recognizing that only a requirement that states use single-member districts remains in place today.]

[Appellants] suggest that, through the Elections Clause, the Framers set aside electoral issues such as the one before us as questions that only Congress can resolve. We do not agree. In two areas—one-person, one-vote and racial gerrymandering—our cases have held that there is a role for the courts with respect to at least some issues that could arise from a State's drawing of congressional districts. See *Wesberry v. Sanders*, 376 U. S. 1 (1964); *Shaw v. Reno*, 509 U. S. 630 (1993).

But the history is not irrelevant. The Framers were aware of electoral districting problems and considered what to do about them. [At] no point was there a suggestion that the federal courts had a role to play. Nor was there any indication that the Framers had ever heard of courts doing such a thing.

[Partisan] gerrymandering claims have proved far more difficult to adjudicate [than one-person, one-vote cases and cases involving racial discrimination]. The basic reason is that, while it is illegal for a jurisdiction to depart from the one-person, one-vote rule, or to engage in racial discrimination in districting, "a jurisdiction may engage in constitutional political gerrymandering." *Hunt v. Cromartie*, 526 U. S. 541, 551 (1999) (citing *Bush v. Vera*, 517 U. S. 952, 968 (1996).

To hold that legislators cannot take partisan interests into account when drawing district lines would essentially countermand the Framers' decision to entrust districting to political entities. The "central problem" is not determining whether a jurisdiction has engaged in partisan gerrymandering. It is "determining when political gerrymandering has gone too far." *Vieth* [*v. Jubelirer*, 541 U. S. 267, 296 (2004) (plurality opinion). The Court here recounted its prior confrontations will challenges to political gerrymandering. In *Davis v. Bandemer*, 478 U. S. 109 (1986)), a majority thought the case was justiciable but splintered over the proper standard to apply. Four Justices (White, Brennan, Marshall, and Blackmun, JJ.) would have required proof of "intentional discrimination against an identifiable political group and an actual discriminatory effect on that group." Two Justices (Powell and Stevens, JJ.) would have focused on "whether the boundaries of the voting districts have been distorted deliberately and arbitrarily to achieve illegitimate ends." But O'Connor, J., joined by Burger, C.J., and Rehnquist, J., would have held that partisan gerrymandering claims pose political questions because the Equal Protection Clause simply "does not supply judicially manageable standards for resolving" them.]

[Eighteen years later, in *Vieth*, Justice Scalia's plurality opinion also would have held challenges to gerrymanders nonjusticiable due to an absence of judicially manageable standards.] Kennedy, J., concurring in the judgment, noted "the lack of comprehensive and neutral principles for drawing electoral boundaries [and] the absence of rules to limit and confine judicial intervention." He nonetheless left open the possibility that "in another case a standard might emerge." Four Justices dissented.

[The] question [in appraising political gerrymandering claims] is one of degree: How to "provid[e] a standard for deciding how much partisan dominance is too much." *League of United Latin American Citizens v. Perry*, 548 U. S. 399, 420 (2006) (opinion of Kennedy, J.). And it is vital in such circumstances that the Court act only in accord with especially clear standards: "With uncertain limits, intervening courts—even when proceeding with best intentions—would risk assuming political, not legal, responsibility for a process that often produces ill will and distrust." *Vieth*, 541 U. S., at 307 (opinion of Kennedy, J.).

[Partisan] gerrymandering claims invariably sound in a desire for proportional representation. * * * "Our cases, however, clearly foreclose any claim that the Constitution requires proportional representation." [Unable] to claim that the Constitution requires proportional representation outright, plaintiffs inevitably ask the courts to make their own political judgment about how much representation particular political parties *deserve*—based on the votes of their supporters—and to rearrange the challenged districts to achieve that end. But federal courts are not equipped to apportion political power as a matter of fairness, nor is there any basis for concluding that they were authorized to do so.

[The] initial difficulty in settling on a "clear, manageable and politically neutral" test for fairness is that it is not even clear what fairness looks like in this context. [Fairness] may mean a greater number of competitive districts. [On] the other hand, perhaps the ultimate objective of a "fairer" share of seats in the congressional delegation is most readily achieved by yielding to the gravitational pull of proportionality and engaging in cracking and packing, to ensure each party its "appropriate" share of "safe" seats. [Or] perhaps fairness should be measured by adherence to "traditional" districting criteria, such as maintaining political subdivisions, keeping communities of interest together, and protecting incumbents.

[Deciding] among just these different visions of fairness (you can imagine many others) poses basic questions that are political, not legal. There are no legal standards discernible in the Constitution for making such judgments, let alone limited and precise standards that are clear, manageable, and politically neutral.

[Even] assuming the court knew which version of fairness to be looking for, there are no discernible and manageable standards for deciding whether there has been a violation. [Appellees] contend that if we can adjudicate one-person, one-vote claims, we can also assess partisan gerrymandering claims. [But] "vote dilution" in the one-person, one-vote cases refers to the idea that each vote must carry equal weight. [That] requirement does not extend to political parties. It does not mean that each party must be influential in proportion to its number of supporters.

Appellees and the dissent propose a number of "tests" for evaluating partisan gerrymandering claims, but none meets the need for a limited and precise standard that is judicially discernible and manageable. And none provides a solid grounding for judges to take the extraordinary step of reallocating power and influence between political parties.

[The District Court in the North Carolina case used a test that involved a "predominant" legislative purpose coupled with a demand for] a showing "that the dilution of the votes of supporters of a disfavored party in a particular district [is] likely to persist in subsequent elections such that an elected representative from the favored party in the district will not feel a need to be responsive to constituents who support the disfavored party."

[The] District Court's "predominant intent" prong is borrowed from the racial gerrymandering context. [If] district lines were drawn for the purpose of separating racial groups, then they are subject to strict scrutiny because "race-based decisionmaking is inherently suspect." But determining that lines were drawn on the basis of partisanship does not indicate that the districting was improper. A permissible intent—securing partisan advantage—does not become constitutionally impermissible, like racial discrimination, when that permissible intent "predominates."

The District Court tried to limit the reach of its test by requiring plaintiffs to show, in addition to predominant partisan intent, that vote dilution "is likely to persist" to such a degree that the elected representative will feel free to ignore the concerns of the supporters of the minority party. But "[t]o allow district courts to strike down apportionment plans on the basis of their prognostications as to the outcome of future elections . . . invites 'findings' on matters as to which neither judges nor anyone else can have any confidence." *Bandemer*, 478 U. S., at 160 (opinion of O'Connor, J.).

[The] District Courts also found partisan gerrymandering claims justiciable under the First Amendment, coalescing around a basic three-part test: proof of intent to burden individuals based on their voting history or party affiliation; an actual burden on political speech or associational rights; and a causal link between the invidious intent and actual burden. [To] begin, there are no restrictions on speech, association, or any other First Amendment activities in the districting plans at issue. [The] plaintiffs' argument is that partisanship in districting should be regarded as simple discrimination against supporters of the opposing party on the basis of political viewpoint. [It] provides no standard for determining when partisan activity goes too far.

As for actual burden, the slight anecdotal evidence found sufficient by the District Courts in these cases shows that this too is not a serious standard for separating constitutional from unconstitutional partisan gerrymandering. [How] much of a decline in voter engagement is enough to constitute a First Amendment burden? How many door knocks must go unanswered? How many petitions unsigned? How many calls for volunteers unheeded

The dissent proposes using a State's own districting criteria as a neutral baseline from which to measure how extreme a partisan gerrymander is. The dissent would have us line up all the possible maps drawn using those criteria according to the partisan distribution they would produce. Distance from the "median" map would indicate whether a particular districting plan harms supporters of one party to an unconstitutional extent.

As an initial matter, it does not make sense to use criteria that will vary from State to State and year to year as the baseline for determining whether a gerrymander violates the Federal Constitution. The degree of partisan advantage that the Constitution tolerates should not turn on criteria offered by the gerrymanderers themselves.

[Even] if we were to accept the dissent's proposed baseline, it would return us to "the original unanswerable question (How much political motivation and effect is too much?)." *Vieth*, 541 U. S., at 296–297 (plurality opinion). Would twenty percent away from the median map be okay? Forty percent? Sixty percent? Why or why not?

[The] dissent argues that there are other instances in law where matters of degree are left to the courts. True enough. But those instances typically involve constitutional or statutory provisions or common law confining and guiding the exercise of judicial discretion. [Here], on the other hand, the Constitution provides no basis whatever to guide the exercise of judicial discretion. [The] only provision in the Constitution that specifically addresses the matter assigns it to the political branches. See Art. I, § 4, cl. 1. [The Court next dismissed arguments based on the Elections Clause and Article I, § 2.]

Excessive partisanship in districting leads to results that reasonably seem unjust. But the fact that such gerrymandering is "incompatible with democratic principles," does not mean that the solution lies with the federal judiciary. [Federal] judges have no license to reallocate political power between the two major political parties, with no plausible grant of authority in the Constitution, and no legal standards to limit and direct their decisions.

[Our] conclusion does not condone excessive partisan gerrymandering. Nor does our conclusion condemn complaints about districting to echo into a void. The States, for example, are actively addressing the issue on a number of fronts. [The Court here described state legislation, state ballot initiatives, and state constitutional amendments to limit partisan gerrymandering.]

[As] noted, the Framers gave Congress the power to do something about partisan gerrymandering in the Elections Clause. [The Court here described several bills introduced in Congress.] We express no view on any of these pending proposals. We simply note that the avenue for reform established by the Framers, and used by Congress in the past, remains open.

* * *

JUSTICE KAGAN, with whom JUSTICES GINSBURG, BREYER, and SOTOMAYOR join, dissenting.

For the first time ever, this Court refuses to remedy a constitutional violation because it thinks the task beyond judicial capabilities. [The] partisan gerrymanders in these cases deprived citizens of the most fundamental of their constitutional rights: the rights to participate equally in the political process, to join with others to advance political beliefs, and to choose their political representatives. [If] left unchecked, gerrymanders like the ones here may irreparably damage our system of government. And checking them is *not* beyond the courts. The majority's abdication comes just when courts across the country, including those below, have coalesced around manageable judicial standards to resolve partisan gerrymandering claims.

[The] majority concedes (really, how could it not?) that gerrymandering is "incompatible with democratic principles." [That] recognition would seem to demand a response. The majority offers two ideas * * *. One is that the political process can deal with the problem—a proposition so dubious on its face that I feel secure in delaying my answer for some time. The other is that political gerrymanders have always been with us. To its credit, the majority does not frame that point as an originalist constitutional argument. After all (as the majority rightly notes), racial and residential gerrymanders were also once with us, but the Court has done something about that fact. The majority's idea instead seems to be that if we have lived with partisan gerrymanders so long, we will survive.

That complacency has no cause. [While] bygone mapmakers may have drafted three or four alternative districting plans, today's mapmakers can generate thousands of possibilities at the touch of a key—and then choose the one giving their party maximum advantage (usually while still meeting traditional districting requirements). The effect is to make gerrymanders far more effective and durable than before, insulating politicians against all but the most titanic shifts in the political tides.

[Partisan] gerrymandering of the kind before us not only subverts democracy (as if that weren't bad enough). It violates individuals' constitutional rights as well. [That] practice implicates the Fourteenth Amendment's Equal Protection Clause. [And] partisan gerrymandering implicates the First Amendment too. That Amendment gives its greatest protection to political beliefs, speech, and association. Yet partisan gerrymanders subject certain voters to "disfavored treatment"—again, counting their votes for less—precisely because of "their voting history [and] their expression of political views." *Vieth*, 541 U. S., at 314 (opinion of Kennedy, J.).

[The] majority never disagrees; it appears to accept the "principle that each person must have an equal say in the election of representatives." And indeed, without this settled and shared understanding that cases like these inflict constitutional injury, the question of whether there are judicially manageable standards for resolving them would never come up.

So the only way to understand the majority's opinion is as follows: In the face of grievous harm to democratic governance and flagrant infringements on individuals' rights—in the face of escalating partisan manipulation whose compatibility with this Nation's values and law no one defends—the majority declines to provide any remedy. [I'll] give the majority this one—and important—thing: It identifies some dangers everyone should want to avoid. Judges should not be apportioning political power based on their own vision of electoral fairness, whether proportional representation or any other. And judges should not be striking down maps left, right, and center, on the view that every smidgen of politics is a smidgen too much. Respect for state legislative processes—and restraint in the exercise of judicial authority—counsels intervention in only egregious cases.

But in throwing up its hands, the majority misses something under its nose: What it says can't be done *has* been done. Over the past several years, federal courts across the country—including, but not exclusively, in the decisions below—have largely converged on a standard for adjudicating partisan gerrymandering claims (striking down both Democratic and Republican districting plans in the process).

[Start] with the standard the lower courts used. [B]oth courts (like others around the country) used basically the same three-part test to decide whether the plaintiffs had made out a vote dilution claim. As many legal standards do, that test has three parts: (1) intent; (2) effects; and (3) causation. First, the plaintiffs challenging a districting plan must prove that state officials' "predominant purpose" in drawing a district's lines was to "entrench [their party] in power" by diluting the votes of citizens favoring its rival. [Justice Kagan here cited *Common Cause v. Rucho*, 318 F. Supp. 3d 777, 805–806 (M.D.N.C. 2018).] Second, the plaintiffs must establish that the lines drawn in fact have the intended effect by "substantially" diluting their votes. [Justice Kagan here cited *Benisek v. Lamone*, 348 F. Supp. 3d 493, 498 (Md. 2018).] And third, if the plaintiffs make those showings, the State must come up with a legitimate, non-partisan justification to save its map. If you are a lawyer, you know that this test looks utterly ordinary. It is the sort of thing courts work with every day.

[The] majority's response to the District Courts' purpose analysis is discomfiting. The majority does not contest the lower courts' findings; how could it? Instead, the majority says that state officials' intent to entrench their party in power is perfectly "permissible," even when it is the predominant factor in drawing district lines. But that is wrong. [W]hen political actors have a specific and predominant intent to entrench themselves in power by manipulating district lines, that goes too far.

[On] to the second step of the analysis, where the plaintiffs must prove that the districting plan substantially dilutes their votes. [Consider] the sort of evidence used in North Carolina first. There, the plaintiffs demonstrated the districting plan's effects mostly by relying on what might be called the "extreme outlier approach." [The] approach—which also has recently been used in Michigan and Ohio litigation—begins by using advanced computing technology to randomly generate a large collection of districting plans that incorporate the State's physical and political geography and meet its declared districting criteria, *except for* partisan gain. [The] further out on the tail, the more extreme the partisan distortion and the more significant the vote dilution.

Using that approach, the North Carolina plaintiffs offered a boatload of alternative districting plans—all showing that the State's map was an out-out-out-outlier. One expert produced 3,000 maps, adhering in the way described above to the districting criteria that the North Carolina redistricting committee had used, other than partisan advantage. To calculate the partisan outcome of those maps, the expert also used the same election data (a composite of seven elections) that [a North Carolina expert] had employed when devising the North Carolina plan in the first instance. [Every] single one of the 3,000 maps would have produced at least one more Democratic House Member than the State's actual map, and 77% would have elected three or four more. [Based] on those and other findings, the District Court determined that the North Carolina plan substantially dilutes the plaintiffs' votes.

Because the Maryland gerrymander involved just one district, the evidence in that case was far simpler—but no less powerful for that. [In] the old Sixth [District], 47% of registered voters were Republicans and only 36% Democrats. But in the new Sixth, 44% of registered voters were Democrats and only 33% Republicans. That reversal of the district's partisan composition translated into four consecutive Democratic victories, including in a wave election year for Republicans (2014). In what was once a party stronghold, Republicans now have little or no chance to elect their preferred candidate. The District Court thus found that the gerrymandered Maryland map substantially dilutes Republicans' votes.

[By] substantially diluting the votes of citizens favoring their rivals, the politicians of one party had succeeded in entrenching themselves in office. They had beat democracy.

The majority's broadest claim, as I've noted, is that this is a price we must pay because judicial oversight of partisan gerrymandering cannot be "politically neutral" or "manageable." [Consider] neutrality first. Contrary to the majority's suggestion, the District Courts did not have to—and in fact did not—choose among competing visions of electoral fairness. That is because they did not try to compare the State's actual map to an "ideally fair" one (whether based on proportional representation or some other criterion). Instead, they looked at the difference between what the State did and what the State would have done if politicians hadn't been intent on partisan gain. Or put differently, the comparator (or baseline or touchstone) is the result not of a judge's philosophizing but of the State's own characteristics and judgments.

[The] majority's sole response misses the point. According to the majority, "it does not make sense to use" a State's own (non-partisan) districting criteria as the baseline from which to measure partisan gerrymandering because those criteria "will vary from State to State and year to year." But that is a virtue, not a vice—a feature, not a bug.

[The] majority's "how much is too much" critique fares no better than its neutrality argument. How about the following for a first-cut answer: This much is too much. By any measure, a map that produces a greater partisan skew than any of 3,000 randomly generated maps (all with the State's political geography and districting criteria built in) reflects "too much" partisanship. Think about what I just said: The absolute worst of 3,001 possible maps. The *only one* that could produce a 10–3 partisan split even as Republicans got a bare majority of the statewide vote. And again: How much is too much? This much is too much: A map that without any evident non-partisan districting reason (to the contrary) shifted the composition of a district from 47% Republicans and 36% Democrats to 33% Republicans and 42% Democrats. A map that in 2011 was responsible for the largest partisan swing of a congressional district in the country.

And if the majority thought that approach too case-specific, it could have used the lower courts' general standard—focusing on "predominant" purpose and "substantial" effects—without fear of indeterminacy. I do not take even the majority to claim that courts are incapable of investigating whether legislators mainly intended to seek partisan advantage.

[Nor] is there any reason to doubt, as the majority does, the competence of courts to determine whether a district map "substantially" dilutes the votes of a rival party's supporters from the everything-but-partisanship baseline described above. [As] this Court recently noted, "the law is full of instances" where a judge's decision rests on "estimating rightly . . . some matter of degree"—including the "substantial[ity]" of risk or harm.

[This] Court has long understood that it has a special responsibility to remedy violations of constitutional rights resulting from politicians' districting decisions. [The] need for judicial review is at its most urgent in cases like these. "For here, politicians' incentives conflict with voters' interests, leaving citizens without any political remedy for their constitutional harms." [*Gill v. Whitford*, 138 S.Ct. 1916, 1941 (2018),] (Kagan, J., concurring). Those harms arise because politicians want to stay in office. No one can look to them for effective relief.

[Here Kagan, J., argued that Congress and state political processes were unlikely to provide an effective remedy After noting that the majority had also recognized state courts as a possible source of relief—since the political question doctrine does not apply to them—she asked:] But what do those courts know that this Court does not? If they can develop and apply neutral and manageable standards to identify unconstitutional gerrymanders, why couldn't we?

[The] practices challenged in these cases imperil our system of government. Part of the Court's role in that system is to defend its foundations. None is more important than free and fair elections. With respect but deep sadness, I dissent.

P. 44, substitute for note 3:

The topic of "judicially manageable standards" is extensively discussed and debated in *Rucho v. Common Cause*, which appears immediately above in this Supplement.

3. CONGRESSIONAL REGULATION OF JUDICIAL POWER

P. 60, at the end of note 9:

Department of Homeland Security v. Thuraissigiam, 140 S.Ct. 1959 (2020), found that a statute precluding habeas corpus review did not violate the Suspension Clause as applied to a noncitizen, apprehended within twenty-five yards of his initial crossing of the U.S. border, who sought to challenge administrative determinations that he had failed to establish a "credible fear of persecution" if returned to his homeland. Alito, J.'s, opinion for the Court reasoned that because the petitioner did not seek a "traditional" release from custody—but rather a "new opportunity to apply for asylum," during the pendency of which since he would have remained in detention—he fell outside the scope of the writ as it existed when the Constitution was adopted. The Court also held that the denial of judicial review did not violate the Due Process Clause in the case of an alien who had neither lawfully entered the United States nor established significant contacts here. Breyer, J., joined by Ginsburg, J., concurred on the narrower ground that even if the petitioner would have had a right to habeas review of some issues bearing on the legality of his detention under the immigration laws, that right would not extend to claims as fact-bound as his. Sotomayor, J., joined by Kagan, J., dissented, affirming that the Suspension Clause entitled the petitioner to review of his claim that administrative officials had applied the wrong legal standard to his case.

CHAPTER 3

DISTRIBUTION OF FEDERAL POWERS: SEPARATION OF POWERS

■ ■ ■

2. CONGRESSIONAL ACTION AFFECTING "PRESIDENTIAL" POWERS

I. DELEGATION OF RULEMAKING POWER

P. 221, before note 2:

(e) *Future of the "intelligible principle" test.* Congress enacted the Sex Offender Registration and Notification Act (SORNA), in order to provide for greater uniformity among state sex-offender registration systems, delegating to the Attorney General "the authority to specify the applicability of [its] requirements" to "offenders convicted before the enactment of" SORNA. In GUNDY v. UNITED STATES, 139 S.Ct. 2116 (2019), the Court rejected a nondelegation challenge to SORNA. KAGAN, J., announced the judgment of the Court and authored an opinion joined by three colleagues rejecting petitioner's contention that the Act "grants the Attorney General plenary power to determine SORNA's applicability to pre-Act offenders. [If] that were so, we would face a nondelegation question. But [the] Attorney General's discretion extends only to considering and addressing feasibility issues," thus satisfying the intelligible principle requirement.

Concurring only in the judgment, ALITO, J., agreed with that conclusion, adding that he would be willing to reconsider the post-*Schechter* nondelegation case law if a majority of the Court were to do so. GORSUCH, J., joined by Roberts, C.J., and Thomas, J., did not wish to wait. He dissented and would have reformed the doctrine by relying on a test that focuses on three questions: "Does the statute assign to the executive only the responsibility to make factual findings? Does it set forth the facts that the executive must consider and the criteria against which to measure them? And most importantly, did Congress, and not the Executive Branch, make the policy judgments? Only then can we fairly say that a statute contains the kind of intelligible principle the Constitution demands." KAVANAUGH, J., did not participate in *Gundy*.

III. APPOINTMENT AND REMOVAL OF OFFICERS

P. 254, before note 5:

(d) SEILA LAW LLC v. CONSUMER FINANCIAL PROTECTION BUREAU, 140 S.Ct. ___, 2020 WL 3492641 (2020), concerned a restriction on the President's power to remove the Director of the Consumer Financial Protection Bureau (CFPB) prior to the expiration of a five-year term. The Supreme Court, per ROBERTS, C.J., held the restriction unconstitutional:

"In the wake of the 2008 financial crisis, Congress [through the Dodd-Frank Act] established the [CFPB], an independent regulatory agency tasked with ensuring that consumer debt products are safe and transparent. In organizing the CFPB, Congress deviated from the structure of nearly every other independent administrative agency in our history. Instead of placing the agency under the leadership of a board with multiple members, Congress provided that the CFPB would be led by a single Director, who serves for a longer term than the President and cannot be removed by the President except for inefficiency, neglect, or malfeasance. The CFPB Director has no boss, peers, or voters to report to. Yet the Director wields vast rulemaking, enforcement, and adjudicatory authority over a significant portion of the U. S. economy. The question before us is whether this arrangement violates the Constitution's separation of powers.

"Our precedents have recognized only two exceptions to the President's unrestricted removal power. In *Humphrey's Executor* we held that Congress could create expert agencies led by a *group* of principal officers removable by the President only for good cause. And in *United States v. Perkins*, 116 U.S. 483 (1886) [which upheld tenure protections for a naval cadet-engineer], and *Morrison* we held that Congress could provide tenure protections to certain *inferior* officers with narrowly defined duties.

"We are now asked to extend these precedents to a new configuration: an independent agency that wields significant executive power and is run by a single individual who cannot be removed by the President unless certain statutory criteria are met. We decline to take that step. While we need not and do not revisit our prior decisions allowing certain limitations on the President's removal power, there are compelling reasons not to extend those precedents to the novel context of an independent agency led by a single Director. Such an agency lacks a foundation in historical practice and clashes with constitutional structure by concentrating power in a unilateral actor insulated from Presidential control."

The Court nonetheless denied relief to the petitioner, a California-based law firm that provided debt-related legal services to clients and that resisted a subpoena from the CFPB on the ground that, in light of the unconstitutional tenure protection for the Director, the agency had no lawful authority. In a portion of his lead opinion joined only by Alito and Kavanaugh, JJ., the Chief Justice rejected petitioner's plea: "The provisions of the Dodd-Frank Act bearing on the CFPB's structure and duties remain fully operative without the offending tenure restriction. Those provisions are capable of functioning independently, and there is nothing in the text or history of the Dodd-Frank Act that demonstrates Congress would have preferred *no* CFPB to a CFPB supervised by the President. Quite the opposite. [The] Dodd-Frank Act contains an express severability clause." Because the Justices who dissented on the merits concurred in the judgment with respect to severability, the petitioner was denied relief but the CFPB Director was rendered subject to removal at will by the President.

THOMAS, J., joined by Gorsuch, J., concurred in the merits: "*Humphrey's Executor* does not comport with the Constitution. [The] Constitution does not permit the creation of officers exercising 'quasi-legislative' and 'quasi-judicial powers' in 'quasi-legislative' and 'quasi-judicial agencies.' No such powers or agencies exist. Congress lacks the authority to delegate its legislative power, and it cannot authorize the use of judicial power by officers acting outside of the bounds of Article III. Nor can Congress create agencies that straddle multiple branches of Government. The Constitution sets out three branches of Government and provides each with a different form of power—legislative, executive, and judicial. [If] any remnant of *Humphrey's Executor* is still standing, it certainly is not enough to justify the numerous, unaccountable independent agencies that currently exercise vast executive power outside the bounds of our constitutional structure."

With respect to the remedy, THOMAS, J., joined by Gorsuch, J., dissented: "The Federal Judiciary does not have the power to excise, erase, alter, or otherwise strike down a statute. And the Court's reference to severability as a 'remedy' is inaccurate. Traditional remedies—like injunctions, declarations, or damages—operate with respect to specific parties, not on legal rules in the abstract [citations and internal quotation marks omitted]."

KAGAN, J., joined by Ginsburg, Breyer, and Sotomayor, JJ., concluded that "*if* the agency's removal provision is unconstitutional, it should be severed," but dissented on the merits: "The majority offers the civics class version of separation of powers—call it the Schoolhouse Rock definition of the phrase. [Yet,] as James Madison stated, the creation of distinct branches 'did not mean that these departments ought to have no partial agency in, or no controul over the acts of each other.' The Federalist No. 47. [The] founding era closed without any agreement that Congress lacked the power to curb the President's removal authority. And as it kept that question open, Congress took the first steps—which would launch a tradition—of distinguishing financial regulators from diplomatic and military officers. The latter mainly helped the President carry out his own constitutional duties in foreign relations and war. The former chiefly carried out statutory duties, fulfilling functions Congress had assigned to their offices. In addressing the new Nation's finances, Congress had begun to use its powers under the Necessary and Proper Clause to design effective administrative institutions. And that included taking steps to insulate certain officers from political influence. As the decades and centuries passed, those efforts picked up steam. Confronting new economic, technological, and social conditions, Congress—and often the President—saw new needs for pockets of independence within the federal bureaucracy. And that was especially so, again, when it came to financial regulation.

"[Congress's] choice to put a single director, rather than a multimember commission, at the CFPB's head violates no principle of separation of powers. [To] make sense on the majority's own terms, the distinction between singular and plural agency heads must rest on a theory about why the former more easily 'slip' from the President's grasp. But [the] opposite is more likely to be true: To the extent that such matters are measurable, individuals are easier than groups to supervise."

4. IMPEACHMENT OF THE PRESIDENT

P. 268, replace the introductory paragraph to Section 4 with the following:

In December 2019, for the third time in U.S. history, the House of Representatives impeached the President, who was then tried by the Senate. In each instance—Andrew Johnson in 1868, William Clinton in 1999, and Donald Trump in 2020—the Senate voted to acquit. A fourth President, Richard Nixon, would almost certainly have been impeached and very likely convicted and removed had he not resigned in 1974. In *Nixon v. United States* Ch. 1, Sec. 2 supra, (which concerned a federal judge with the same surname as the former President) the Supreme Court ruled that matters respecting congressional impeachments present nonjusticiable political questions. Thus, no judicial opinions address any of the important constitutional questions that may arise. The following notes consider some of these:

CHAPTER 4

STATE POWER TO REGULATE

■ ■ ■

2. BASIC DOCTRINAL PRINCIPLES AND THEIR APPLICATION

I. STATUTES THAT DISCRIMINATE ON THEIR FACES AGAINST INTERSTATE COMMERCE

P. 289, before *Maine v. Taylor*:

TENNESSEE WINE AND SPIRITS RETAILERS ASS'N v. TENNESSEE ALCOHOLIC BEVERAGE COMM'N, 139 S.Ct. 2449 (2019), invalidated a Tennessee statute that imposed a two-year duration-of-residency requirement for licenses to own and operate liquor stores. Writing for a 7–2 majority, ALITO, J., began by noting recent criticisms of dormant Commerce Clause doctrine, but he responded by citing original historical expectations that the Constitution would provide "protection against a broad swathe of state protectionist measures." Within the existing doctrinal framework, Tennessee's principal defense of its discriminatory residency test rested on § 2 of the Twenty-first Amendment, which provides that "[t]he transportation or importation into any State, Territory, or possession of the United States for delivery or use therein of intoxicating liquors, in violation of the laws thereof, is hereby prohibited." Despite some early judicial suggestions that § 2 gave the states plenary control over all matters involving alcohol, the Court had subsequently recognized that it must "scrutinize state alcohol laws for compliance with many constitutional provisions," including the First and Fourteenth Amendments. With respect to the dormant Commerce Clause, examination of relevant history "convince[s] us that the aim of § 2 was not to give states a free hand to restrict the importation of alcohol." GORSUCH, J., joined by Thomas, J., dissented: "[T]hose who ratified the [Twenty-first] Amendment wanted the States to be able to regulate the sale of liquor free of judicial meddling under the dormant Commerce Clause."

CHAPTER 6

PROTECTION OF INDIVIDUAL RIGHTS: DUE PROCESS, THE BILL OF RIGHTS, AND UNENUMERATED RIGHTS

■ ■ ■

1. APPLICABILITY OF THE BILL OF RIGHTS TO THE STATES; NATURE AND SCOPE OF FOURTEENTH AMENDMENT DUE PROCESS

II. IS THE BILL OF RIGHTS INCORPORATED "JOT-FOR-JOT"?

Pp. 418–20, delete the note on *Baldwin*, *Williams*, and *Apodaca*:

III. IN *MCDONALD V. CITY OF CHICAGO*, THE COURT LOOKS BACK ON ITS "INCORPORATION" OF BILL OF RIGHTS GUARANTEES

P. 421, delete footnote 14 and insert immediately before IV:

In TIMBS v. INDIANA, 139 S.Ct. 682 (2019), GINSBURG, J., wrote for the Court that "the historical and logical case for concluding that the Fourteenth Amendment incorporates the Excessive Fines Clause is overwhelming." The Court rejected the State's contention that the Fourteenth Amendment did not incorporate the Clause's application to civil *in rem* forfeitures that are at least partly punitive. The decision was unanimous in result, but THOMAS, J., concurred only in the judgment. Adhering to a view he expressed in *McDonald* (Sec. 7 infra), he would have relied on the Fourteenth Amendment's Privileges or Immunities Clause as the basis for incorporation. Concurring in the majority opinion, GORSUCH, J., "acknowledge[d]" that "[a]s an original matter . . . the appropriate vehicle for incorporation may well be the Fourteenth Amendment's Privileges or Immunities Clause, rather than, as this Court has long assumed, the Due Process Clause." However, he continued, "nothing in this case turns on that question, and, regardless of the precise vehicle, there can be no serious doubt that the Fourteenth Amendment requires the States to respect the freedom from excessive fines enshrined in the Eighth Amendment."

RAMOS v. LOUISIANA, 140 S.Ct. 1390 (2020), presented the question whether the Sixth Amendment requirement of a unanimous twelve-person jury in serious criminal cases is incorporated. GORSUCH, J., wrote for the Court: "In 48 States and federal court, a single juror's vote to acquit is enough to prevent a conviction. But not in Louisiana. Along with Oregon, Louisiana has long punished people based on 10-to-2 verdicts. [Wherever] we might look to determine what the term 'trial by an impartial jury trial' meant at the time of the Sixth Amendment's adoption—whether it's the common law, state practices in the founding era, or opinions and treatises written soon afterward—the answer is unmistakable. A jury must reach a unanimous verdict in order to convict.

"There can be no question either that the Sixth Amendment's unanimity requirement applies to state and federal criminal trials equally. This Court has long explained that the Sixth Amendment right to a jury trial is 'fundamental to the American scheme of justice' and incorporated against the States under the Fourteenth Amendment. This Court has long explained, too, that incorporated provisions of the Bill of Rights bear the same content when asserted against States as they do when asserted against the federal government. So if the Sixth Amendment's right to a jury trial requires a unanimous verdict to support a conviction in federal court, it requires no less in state court.

"How, despite these seemingly straightforward principles, have Louisiana's and Oregon's laws managed to hang on for so long? It turns out that the Sixth Amendment's otherwise simple story took a strange turn. [In] *Apodaca* v. *Oregon,* 406 U.S. 404 (1972), [four] dissenting Justices would not have hesitated to strike down the States' laws, recognizing that the Sixth Amendment requires unanimity and that this guarantee is fully applicable against the States under the Fourteenth Amendment. But a four-Justice plurality [declared] that the real question [was] whether unanimity serves an important 'function' in 'contemporary society.' [Justice] Powell agreed that, as a matter of 'history and precedent, the Sixth Amendment requires a unanimous jury verdict to convict.' But, on the other hand, he argued that the Fourteenth Amendment does not render this guarantee against the federal government fully applicable against the States. In this way, Justice Powell doubled down on his belief in 'dual-track' incorporation—the idea that a single right can mean two different things depending on whether it is being invoked against the federal or a state government.

"[Even] if we accepted the premise that *Apodaca* established a precedent, no one on the Court today is prepared to say it was rightly decided, and *stare decisis* isn't supposed to be the art of methodically ignoring what everyone knows to be true. [Louisiana and Oregon] credibly claim that the number of nonunanimous felony convictions still on direct appeal are somewhere in the hundreds, and retrying or plea bargaining these cases will surely impose a cost. But new rules of criminal procedures usually do, often affecting significant numbers of pending cases across the whole country."

SOTOMAYOR and KAVANAUGH, JJ., each wrote a partial concurrence explaining their respective views of *stare decisis*. THOMAS, J., concurred in the judgment, reiterating his view that the Fourteenth Amendment's Privileges or Immunities Clause provides the proper basis for incorporation. *See McDonald, infra*, Sec. 7.

ALITO, J., joined by Roberts, C.J., and Kagan, J., dissented on *stare decisis* grounds: The Court "imposes a potentially crushing burden on the courts and criminal justice systems of [Louisiana and Oregon]. Whatever one may think about the correctness of [*Apodaca*], it has elicited enormous and entirely reasonable reliance. And before this Court decided to intervene, the decision appeared to have little practical importance going forward. Louisiana has now abolished non-unanimous verdicts, and Oregon seemed on the verge of doing the same until the Court intervened."

IV. HOW MUCH MORE SPECIFIC ARE PROVISIONS OF THE BILL OF RIGHTS THAN DUE PROCESS GENERALLY? THE CASE OF BODILY EXTRACTIONS

P. 425, add a note after 2:

3. ***Mandatory vaccination.*** As this Supplement goes to press, scientists around the world are testing potential vaccines to provide immunity against COVID-19, the disease caused by the coronavirus that first emerged in humans in late 2019. Vaccines protect the individuals to whom they are administered, but even an effective vaccine will not be 100 percent effective, and some vulnerable people will be unable to receive the vaccine due to underlying medical conditions. Nonetheless, unvaccinated individuals can be protected by a vaccine administered to others through *herd immunity*: when a sufficiently high proportion of the community has been vaccinated or acquired immunity from the disease itself, the contagion ceases to spread because it does not encounter sufficiently many vulnerable hosts. The portion of the population that must be vaccinated for a community to achieve herd immunity depends on the vaccine's effectiveness and the disease's contagiousness. However, given substantial numbers of Americans who express a personal objection to vaccination, herd immunity might not be achievable without a government mandate. Would such a mandate violate a right to bodily autonomy?

JACOBSON v. MASSACHUSETTS, 197 U.S. 11 (1905), per HARLAN, J., upheld a criminal conviction of the defendant for refusal to submit to a free state-mandated vaccination against smallpox: The defendant relied on "the general theory of those of the medical profession who attach little or no value to vaccination as a means of preventing the spread of smallpox, or who think that vaccination causes other diseases of the body. What everybody knows, the court must know, and therefore the state court judicially knew, as this court knows, that an opposite theory accords with the common belief and is maintained by high medical authority. We must assume that, when the statute in question was passed, the legislature of Massachusetts was not unaware of these opposing theories, and was compelled, of necessity, to choose between them. [The] state legislature proceeded upon the theory which recognized vaccination as at least an effective, if not the best, known way in which to meet and suppress the evils of a smallpox epidemic that imperiled an entire population. [Whatever] may be thought of the expediency of this statute, it cannot be affirmed to be, beyond question, in palpable conflict with the Constitution. Nor, in view of the methods employed to stamp out the disease of smallpox, can anyone confidently assert that the means prescribed by the State to that end has no real or substantial relation to the protection of the public health and the public safety."

Note that *Jacobson* was decided in the same year as *Lochner*, whose author, Peckham, J., along with Brewer, J., dissented without opinion. Does *Jacobson* apply the same test as modern bodily autonomy cases? If not, is it nonetheless still good law?

2. REPRODUCTIVE FREEDOM

P. 442, add a paragraph at the end of footnote 14:

McCorvey's story took one final surprise turn. Before her death in February 2017, she issued what she sardonically called a "deathbed confession" that she was never really pro-life after all. Footage was included in a television documentary that premiered on the FX Network in 2020. *AKA Jane Roe* also showed financial records indicating that McCorvey had been paid nearly half a million dollars by pro-life organizations and individuals.

Purported Health Regulations

P. 484, add a new note after 2:

3. ***Balancing and stare decisis (revisited).*** According to the *Whole Woman's Health* majority, *Casey* "requires that courts consider the burdens a law imposes on abortion access together with the benefits those laws confer" in determining whether the former are "undue." Does *Casey* as construed by *Whole Woman's Health* thus establish a balancing test? That question divided the Court in JUNE MEDICAL SERVICES L. L. C. v. RUSSO, 140 S.Ct. ___, 2020 WL 3492640 (2020). BREYER, J., again delivered the judgment, although here, unlike in *Whole Woman's Health*, he spoke only for a plurality consisting of himself and Ginsburg, Sotomayor, and Kagan, JJ.

The Court considered "the constitutionality of a Louisiana statute, Act 620, that is almost word-for-word identical to Texas' admitting-privileges law. As in *Whole Woman's Health*, the District Court found that the statute offers no significant health benefit. It found that conditions on admitting privileges common to hospitals throughout the State have made and will continue to make it impossible for abortion providers to obtain conforming privileges for reasons that have nothing to do with the State's asserted interests in promoting women's health and safety. And it found that this inability places a substantial obstacle in the path of women seeking an abortion. As in *Whole Woman's Health*, the substantial obstacle the Act imposes, and the absence of any health-related benefit, led the District Court to conclude that the law imposes an undue burden and is therefore unconstitutional." Because the appeals court nonetheless found distinctions between the Louisiana and Texas laws in their application, it upheld Act 620. The Court reversed, invalidating it as indistinguishable from the Texas law.

Crediting the district court's factual findings as not clearly erroneous, the plurality observed that Act 620 "would leave Louisiana with just one clinic with one provider to serve the 10,000 women annually who seek abortions in the State. Working full time in New Orleans, [that one doctor, identified in the record as] Doe 5 would be able to absorb no more than about 30% of the annual demand for abortions in Louisiana. And because Doe 5 does not perform abortions beyond 18 weeks, women between 18 weeks and the state legal limit of 20 weeks would have little or no way to exercise their constitutional right to an abortion.

"Those women not altogether prevented from obtaining an abortion would face other burdens. As in *Whole Woman's Health*, the reduction in abortion providers caused by Act 620 would inevitably mean 'longer waiting times, and increased crowding.' The District Court heard testimony that delays in obtaining an abortion increase the risk that a woman will experience complications from the procedure and may make it impossible for her to choose a noninvasive medication abortion.

"Even if they obtain an appointment at a clinic, women who might previously have gone to a clinic in Baton Rouge or Shreveport would face increased driving distances. New Orleans is nearly a five hour drive from Shreveport; it is over an hour from Baton Rouge; and Baton Rouge is more than four hours from Shreveport. The impact of those increases would be magnified by Louisiana's requirement that every woman undergo an ultrasound and receive mandatory counseling at least 24 hours before an abortion. A Shreveport resident seeking an abortion who might previously have obtained care at one of that city's local clinics would either have to spend nearly 20 hours driving back and forth to Doe 5's clinic twice, or else find overnight lodging in New Orleans. As the District Court stated, both experts and laypersons testified that the burdens of this increased travel would fall disproportionately on poor women, who are least able to absorb them.

"[The] District Court found that the admitting-privileges requirement serves no 'relevant credentialing function.' [H]ospitals can, and do, deny admitting privileges for reasons unrelated to a doctor's ability safely to perform abortions. And Act 620's requirement that physicians obtain privileges at a hospital within 30 miles of the place where they perform abortions further constrains providers for reasons that bear no relationship to competence. [Further,] the District Court found that the admitting-privileges requirement 'does not conform to prevailing medical standards and will not improve the safety of abortion in Louisiana.' As in *Whole Woman's Health*, the [State] introduced no evidence 'showing that patients have better outcomes when their physicians have admitting privileges' or 'of any instance in which an admitting privileges requirement would have helped even one woman obtain better treatment.'

"[This] case is similar to, nearly identical with, *Whole Woman's Health*. And the law must consequently reach a similar conclusion. Act 620 is unconstitutional."

ROBERTS, C.J., concurred in the judgment: "I joined the dissent in *Whole Woman's Health* and continue to believe that the case was wrongly decided. The question today however is not whether *Whole Woman's Health* was right or wrong, but whether to adhere to it in deciding the present case. [The] legal doctrine of *stare decisis* requires us, absent special circumstances, to treat like cases alike. The Louisiana law imposes a burden on access to abortion just as severe as that imposed by the Texas law, for the same reasons. Therefore Louisiana's law cannot stand under our precedents.

"*Stare decisis* ('to stand by things decided') is the legal term for fidelity to precedent. Black's Law Dictionary 1696 (11th ed. 2019). It has long been "an established rule to abide by former precedents, where the same points come again in litigation; as well to keep the scale of justice even and steady, and not liable to waver with every new judge's opinion.' 1 W. Blackstone, Commentaries on the Laws of England 69 (1765). This principle is grounded in a basic humility that recognizes today's legal issues are often not so different from the questions of yesterday and that we are not the first ones to try to answer them. Because the 'private stock of reason . . . in each man is small, . . . individuals would do better to avail themselves of the general bank and capital of nations and of ages.' 3 Edmund Burke, *Reflections on the Revolution in France* 110 (1790).

"Adherence to precedent is necessary to 'avoid an arbitrary discretion in the courts.' *The Federalist* No. 78, p. 529 (J. Cooke ed. 1961) (A. Hamilton). The constraint of precedent distinguishes the judicial "method and philosophy from those of the political and legislative process." Robert Jackson, *Decisional Law and Stare Decisis*, 30 A.B.A.J. 334 (1944).

"The doctrine also brings pragmatic benefits. Respect for precedent 'promotes the evenhanded, predictable, and consistent development of legal principles, fosters reliance on judicial decisions, and contributes to the actual and perceived integrity of the judicial process.' *Payne v. Tennessee*, 501 U.S. 808 (1991). It is the 'means by which we ensure that the law will not merely change erratically, but will develop in a principled and intelligible fashion.' *Vasquez v. Hillery*, 474 U.S. 254 (1986). In that way, 'stare decisis is an old friend of the common lawyer.' Jackson, *supra*

"*Stare decisis* is not an 'inexorable command.' *Ramos* v. *Louisiana*, *supra* (internal quotation marks omitted). But for precedent to mean anything, the doctrine must give way only to a rationale that goes beyond whether the case was decided correctly. The Court accordingly considers additional factors before overruling a precedent, such as its administrability, its fit with subsequent factual and legal developments, and the reliance interests that the precedent has engendered.

"*Stare decisis* principles also determine how we handle a decision that itself departed from the cases that came before it. In those instances, '[r]emaining true to an 'intrinsically sounder' doctrine established in prior cases better serves the values of *stare decisis* than would following' the recent departure. *Adarand Constructors, Inc.* v. *Peña*, Ch.9, Sec. 2, V(A) (plurality opinion). *Stare decisis* is pragmatic and contextual, not 'a mechanical formula of adherence to the latest decision.' *Helvering v. Hallock*, 309 U.S. 106 (1940).

"[The parties] agree that the undue burden standard announced in *Casey* provides the appropriate framework to analyze Louisiana's law. Neither party has asked us to reassess the constitutional validity of that standard. [Under] *Casey*, the State may not impose an undue burden on the woman's ability to obtain an abortion.

"[The] Court in *Whole Woman's Health* added the following observation [to its recitation of the *Casey* standard]: 'The rule announced in *Casey* . . . requires that courts consider the burdens a law imposes on abortion access together with the benefits those laws confer.' The plurality repeats today that the undue burden standard requires courts 'to weigh the law's asserted benefits against the burdens it imposes on abortion access.'

"[Under] such [grand balancing] tests, 'equality of treatment is . . . impossible to achieve; predictability is destroyed; judicial arbitrariness is facilitated; judicial courage is impaired.' Antonin Scalia, *The Rule of Law as a Law of Rules*, 56 U.Chi.L.Rev. 1175 (1989). In this context, courts applying a balancing test would be asked in essence to weigh the State's interests in 'protecting the potentiality of human life' and the health of the woman, on the one hand, against the woman's liberty interest in defining her 'own concept of existence, of meaning, of the universe, and of the mystery of human life' on the other. *Casey*. There is no plausible sense in which anyone, let alone this Court, could objectively assign weight to such imponderable values and no meaningful way to compare them if there were.

"[Nothing] about *Casey* suggested that a weighing of costs and benefits of an abortion regulation was a job for the courts. [The] upshot of *Casey* is clear: The several restrictions that did not impose a substantial obstacle were constitutional, while the restriction that did impose a substantial obstacle was unconstitutional. To be sure, the Court at times discussed the benefits of the regulations, including when it distinguished spousal notification from parental consent. But in the context of *Casey*'s governing standard, these benefits were not placed on a scale opposite the law's burdens. Rather, *Casey* discussed benefits in considering the threshold requirement that the State have a 'legitimate purpose' and that the law be 'reasonably related to that goal.' So long as that showing is made, the only question for a court is whether a law has the 'effect of placing a substantial obstacle in the path of a woman seeking an abortion of a nonviable fetus.' *Casey* repeats that 'substantial obstacle' standard nearly verbatim no less than 15 times.

"[Nonetheless, w]e should respect the statement in *Whole Woman's Health* that it was applying the undue burden standard of *Casey*. [Here] the plurality expressly acknowledges that we are not considering how to analyze an abortion regulation that does not present a substantial obstacle. [In] this case, *Casey*'s requirement of finding a substantial obstacle before invalidating an abortion regulation is therefore a sufficient basis for the decision, as it was in *Whole Woman's Health*. In neither case, nor in *Casey* itself, was there call for consideration of a regulation's benefits, and nothing in *Casey* commands such consideration. Under principles of *stare decisis*, I agree with the plurality that the determination in *Whole Woman's Health* that Texas's law imposed a substantial obstacle requires the same determination about Louisiana's law. Under those same principles, I would adhere to the holding of *Casey*, requiring a substantial obstacle before striking down an abortion regulation."

THOMAS, J., dissented chiefly on the ground that the plaintiffs should be denied third-party standing. On the merits, he added that the Court's abortion "decisions created the right to abortion out of whole cloth, without a shred of support from the Constitution's text. Our abortion precedents are grievously wrong and should be overruled."

ALITO, J., joined in full by Gorsuch, J., and in different parts by Thomas and Kavanaugh, JJ., dissented. In portions of his dissent in which all the dissenters concurred, he agreed with Chief Justice Roberts that *Casey* "rules out the balancing test adopted in *Whole Woman's Health*. *Whole Woman's Health* simply misinterpreted *Casey* [and] should be overruled insofar as it changed the *Casey* test. Unless *Casey* is reexamined—and Louisiana has not asked us to do that—the test it adopted should remain the governing standard.

"[In] any event, contrary to the view taken by the plurality and (seemingly) by the Chief Justice, there is ample evidence in the record showing that admitting privileges help to protect the health of women by ensuring that physicians who perform abortions meet a higher standard of competence than is shown by the mere possession of a license to practice. In deciding whether to grant admitting privileges, hospitals typically undertake a rigorous investigative process to ensure that a doctor is responsible and competent and has the training and experience needed to perform the procedures for which the privileges are sought. [Both] the plurality and the Chief Justice err in concluding that the admitting-privileges requirement serves no valid purpose.

"They also err in their assessment of Act 620's likely effect on access to abortion. [Because] the Louisiana law was not allowed to go into effect for any appreciable time, it was necessary for the District Court to predict what its effects would be. Attempting to do that, the court apparently concluded that none of the doctors who currently perform abortions in the State would be replaced if the admitting privileges requirement forced them to leave abortion practice. [The] finding was based on a fundamentally flawed test. In attempting to ascertain how many of the doctors who perform abortions in the State would have to leave abortion practice for lack of admitting privileges, the District Court received evidence in a variety of forms—some live testimony, but also deposition transcripts, declarations, and even letters from counsel— about the doctors' unsuccessful efforts to obtain privileges. The District Court considered whether these doctors had proceeded in 'good faith'; it found that they all met that standard; and it therefore concluded that the law would leave the State with very few abortion providers. [However, w]hen the District Court made its assessment of the doctors' 'good faith,' enforcement of Act 620 had been preliminarily enjoined, and the doctors surely knew that enforcement would be permanently barred if the lawsuit was successful. Thus, the doctors had everything to lose and nothing to gain by obtaining privileges."

GORSUCH, J., dissented on multiple grounds, including an objection that in crediting the district court's findings, the Court slighted the state legislature: "Act 620's admitting privileges requirement for abortion providers tracks longstanding state laws governing physicians who perform relatively low-risk procedures like colonoscopies, Lasik eye surgeries, and steroid injections at ambulatory surgical centers. In fact, the Louisiana legislature passed Act 620 only after extensive hearings at which experts detailed how the Act would promote safer abortion treatment—by providing 'a more thorough evaluation mechanism of physician competency,' promoting 'continuity of care' following abortion, enhancing inter-physician communication, and preventing patient abandonment."

Agreeing with the Chief Justice regarding balancing, Justice Gorsuch added that "the legal standard the plurality applies when it comes to admitting privileges for abortion clinics turns out to be exactly the sort of all-things-considered balancing of benefits and burdens this Court has long rejected. Really, it's little more than the judicial version of a hunter's stew: Throw in anything that looks interesting, stir, and season to taste.

"[The] plurality sides with the district court in concluding that the time and cost some women might have to endure to obtain an abortion outweighs the benefits of Act 620. Perhaps the plurality sees that answer as obvious, given its apparent conclusion that the Act would offer the public no benefits of any kind. But for its test to provide any helpful guidance, it must be capable of resolving cases the plurality can't so easily dismiss. Suppose, for example, a factfinder credited the State's evidence of medical benefit, finding that a small number of women would obtain safer medical care if the law went into effect. But suppose the same factfinder *also* credited a plaintiff's evidence of burden, finding that a large number of women would have to endure longer wait times and farther drives, and that a very small number of women would be unable to obtain an abortion at all. How is a judge supposed to balance, say, a few women's emergency hysterectomies against many women spending extra hours travelling to a clinic? The plurality's test offers no guidance. Nor can it. The benefits and burdens are incommensurable, and they do not teach such things in law school."

KAVANAUGH, J., also briefly dissented separately, expressing agreement with the conclusion of Justice Alito "that the Court should remand the case for a new trial and additional factfinding under the appropriate legal standards."

7. THE RIGHT TO KEEP AND BEAR ARMS

P. 587, immediately before Section 8:

NEW YORK STATE RIFLE & PISTOL ASS'N v. CITY OF NEW YORK, 140 S.Ct. 1525 (2020), involved a challenge to a New York City rule restricting the transport of firearms outside of the city, including to shooting ranges and competitions. The city changed the rule before the case reached the Supreme Court, which accordingly dismissed the case as moot in a brief *per curiam* opinion.

ALITO, J, joined by Gorsuch and Thomas, JJ., dissented and would have reached the merits: "We deal here with the same core Second Amendment right [recognized in *Heller* and *McDonald*], the right to keep a handgun in the home for self-defense. [A] necessary concomitant of this right is the right to take a gun outside the home for certain purposes. One of these is to take a gun for maintenance or repair. [Another] is to take a gun outside the home in order to transfer ownership lawfully. [And] still another is to take a gun to a range in order to gain and maintain the skill necessary to use it responsibly."

KAVANAUGH, J., agreed with the *per curiam*'s mootness holding, but concurred to express agreement as well with the dissent's discussion of the merits: "I share Justice Alito's concern that some federal and state courts may not be properly applying *Heller* and *McDonald*. The Court should address that issue soon . . . ."

8. THE DEATH PENALTY AND RELATED PROBLEMS: CRUEL AND UNUSUAL PUNISHMENT

IV. ADDITIONAL CONSTITUTIONAL LIMITS ON IMPOSING SEVERE PUNISHMENT

P. 608, after the final paragraph:

In FORD v. WAINSRIGHT, 477 U.S. 399 (1986), the Supreme Court, per MARSHALL, J., held that the Eighth Amendment forbids executing a prisoner who has "lost his sanity" after sentencing. In MADISON v. ALABAMA, 139 S.Ct. 718 (2019), a 5–3 majority of the Court, per KAGAN, J., applied *Ford* in holding that a prisoner's mere failure to remember committing his crime does not preclude execution but dementia that renders him "unable to rationally understand the reasons for his sentence" does. The Court remanded for application of this standard. ALITO, J., joined by Thomas and Gorsuch, JJ., dissented on the grounds that only the memory question was properly before the Court and that, in any event, the state court had applied the correct standard to the dementia question.

P. 614, before Section 9:

In BUCKLEW v. PRECYTHE, 139 S.Ct. 1112 (2019), a prisoner argued that Missouri's one-drug protocol would be unconstitutional as applied to him because vascular tumors in his head, neck, and throat posed a substantial risk of excruciating pain during the execution. GORSUCH, J., writing for a 5–4 Court, rejected the claim on the ground that in as-applied no less than facial challenges to a method of execution the challenger bears the burden of identifying a " 'feasible, readily implemented' alternative procedure that would 'significantly reduce a substantial risk of severe pain' " (quoting *Glossip* plurality opinion). According to the majority, execution by nitrogen hypoxia, the alternative method to which the prisoner eventually pointed, did not satisfy this standard. BREYER, J., joined by Ginsburg, Sotomayor, and Kagan, JJ., dissented on multiple grounds, including the contention that as-applied challenges should be treated differently from facial ones because the former do not undercut any legislative judgment: "It is impossible to believe that Missouri's legislature, when adopting lethal injection, considered the possibility that it would cause prisoners to choke on their own blood for up to several minutes before they die."

CHAPTER 7

FREEDOM OF EXPRESSION
AND ASSOCIATION

■ ■ ■

1. THE SCOPE AND STRENGTH OF
THE FIRST AMENDMENT

I. ADVOCACY OF ILLEGAL ACTION

D. A Modern "Restatement"

P. 680, at end of note 8:

In NIEVES v. BARTLETT, 139 S.Ct. 1715 (2019), the Court seemingly narrowed its conclusion in *Lozman*. In *Nieves*, Russell Bartlett had been arrested for disorderly conduct and resisting arrest in the context of an altercation that took place during an Alaska sports festival "known for both extreme sports and extreme alcohol consumption." The criminal charges against Bartlett were ultimately dismissed, whereupon he sued the arresting officers, including Nieves, under 42 U.S.C. § 1983, claiming that his arrest was in retaliation for his speech, in particular his comments during the altercation about the behavior of the arresting officers. The district court having determined that the officers had probable cause to arrest Bartlett, the issue then turned on the question of the burden of proof in a retaliatory arrest claim based on an allegation that the arrest was in retaliation for engaging in otherwise protected speech.

Writing for the Court, ROBERTS, C.J., noted that *Lozman* was based on "unusual circumstances" and that *Nieves v. Bartlett* presented a "more representative case." And in this more representative case, the Court concluded that the plaintiff must establish a causal connection between the impermissible retaliatory motive and the subsequent arrest, and that the causal connection must be of the "but for" variety. Noting that "protected speech is often a legitimate consideration when deciding whether to make an arrest," the Court concluded that the presence of probable cause would generally (*Lozman* presenting the narrow exception of the presence of probable cause under circumstances in which it could objectively be shown that otherwise similarly situated individuals not engaged in protected speech would not have been arrested) defeat a retaliatory arrest claim. When there was no probable cause for the arrest, it would still be necessary for the plaintiff to show that the retaliation was a "substantial or motivating factor behind the arrest." If a plaintiff were able to make such a showing, then the burden of proof would shift to the defendant to show that the arrest would have been initiated without respect to the retaliation.

THOMAS, J., concurring in part and concurring in the judgment, would have rejected even the *Lozman* exception. GORSUCH, J., concurring in part and dissenting in part, stressed that for him the presence of probable cause was relevant to a retaliatory arrest claim, but that it was not nearly as conclusive as it appeared to be for the majority. GINSBURG, J., concurring in part and dissenting in part, also objected to the weight given by the majority to the presence of probable cause. And SOTOMAYOR, J., dissenting, also took issue with the almost conclusive role the majority gave to the presence of probable cause, believing, with Ginsburg, J., that the proper approach was one drawn from *Mt. Healthy City Bd. of Educ. v. Doyle*, 429 U.S. 274 (1977), in which "the plaintiff bears the burden of demonstrating that unconstitutional animus was a motivating factor for an adverse action; the burden then shifts to the defendant to demonstrate that, even without any impetus to retaliate, the defendant would have taken the action complained of."

2. THE PROBLEM OF CONTENT REGULATION

P. 833, at end of note 3:

Two Terms after *Matal v. Tam*, the Court revisited the issue of offensive trademarks in IANCU v. BRUNETTI, 139 S.Ct. 2294 (2019), where the Court held that the Lanham Act's prohibition on registration for "immoral or scandalous" trademarks constituted impermissible viewpoint-based discrimination. At issue was an attempted registration of the trademark FUCT by the clothing manufacturer who used these four letters, allegedly pronounced as four separate letters, as the brand name for its clothing line. Relying substantially on *Matal*, the Court, with KAGAN, J., writing the majority opinion, rejected the argument that the "immoral or scandalous" standard was merely a viewpoint-neutral restriction on the manner in which a point of view could be expressed but was not itself a viewpoint-based standard. The Court also rejected the government's argument that the statutory criteria were not facially invalid but only that there had been errors in application by trademark examiners in applying the criteria, and rejected as well the argument that the statute could be subject to a saving narrowing construction.

Concurring, ALITO, J., noted that a redrafted statute precluding registration of "vulgar terms" could likely be valid, but that "[v]iewpoint discrimination is poison to a free society. But in many countries with constitutions or legal traditions that claim to protect freedom of speech, serious viewpoint discrimination is now tolerated, and such discrimination has become increasingly prevalent in this country. At a time when free speech is under attack, it is especially important for this Court to remain firm on the principle that the First Amendment does not tolerate viewpoint discrimination."

ROBERTS, C.J., BREYER, J., and SOTOMAYOR, J., each wrote opinions concurring in part and dissenting in part. All three agreed with the majority that the "immoral" component in the statutory standard was impermissibly viewpoint-based, but that it could be excised by the Court, leaving the "scandalous" element in place, an element that for all three of these concurring justices was sufficiently close a restriction on only the lewd or the profane that it could be understood as not being viewpoint-based. Justice Breyer's opinion also objected to the Court's continuing reliance on rigid First Amendment categories, believing that the Court should focus on the "more basic proportionality question" whether the harm to the First Amendment's interests was disproportionate to the government's regulatory objectives.

I. "HATE SPEECH" AND THE *SKOKIE* CONTROVERSY

P. 882, after *Reed v. Gilbert*:

The Court's divisions about the scope and strength of the bar against content regulation continued in the 2019 Term. BARR v. AMERICAN ASSOCIATION OF POLITICAL CONSULTANTS, INC., 140 S.Ct. ___, 2020 WL 3633780 (2020), produced a decision whose lack of a majority opinion underscored the way in which content regulation doctrine remains in flux and contested.

The case concerned the Telephone Consumer Protection Act of 1991, which in relevant part prohibits virtually all robocalls to cell phones. In 2015, however, Congress amended the Act to exclude from the robocall prohibition calls made to collect a government debt, a category including many student loans and home mortgages. An association of political consultants, many of whose members wished to be able to make political robocalls to cell phones, challenged the amended Act, arguing that its preference for government debt-collection robocalls over political robocalls violated the First Amendment.

In a fractured set of opinions, the Court agreed that the amended Act engaged in constitutionally impermissible content discrimination in violation of the First Amendment, and that the appropriate remedy, affirming the Fourth Circuit decision below, was to sever the constitutionally flawed government debt exception, leaving the overall robocall prohibition, without the exception, in place.

KAVANAUGH, J., writing for a plurality including himself, Roberts, C.J. Thomas, J. (in part), and Alito, J., relied heavily on *Reed* in concluding that the exception for government debt collection "impermissibly favored [government] debt-collection speech over political and other speech," and thus constituted unconstitutional content discrimination. Emphasizing that "content-based laws are subject to strict scrutiny," Justice Kavanaugh reiterated *Reed*'s conclusion that strict scrutiny applied to laws that "single[ ] out specific subject matter for differential treatment." For the plurality, the fact that the regulation was part of a broader regulatory scheme regulating the economic activity of debt collection was of no moment, because here the regulation of speech was not merely incidental to a broader regulatory program. Quoting *Sorrell v. IMS*, *supra*, Justice Kavanaugh argued that "the law here ['does] not simply have an effect on speech, but is directed at certain content and is aimed at particular speakers' "

Having concluded that strict scrutiny was the applicable standard, the merits of the controversy were essentially over, with even the government having conceded that "collecting government debt" was not the kind of interest that would satisfy strict scrutiny. But the question remained about the remedy. For the plurality, traditional severability principles were applicable, the most important of which, in this context, was the "presumption of severability." Applying that presumption and finding that the robocall prohibition without the government debt collection exception was "capable of functioning independently," *Murphy v. National Collegiate Athletic Association,* 138 S.Ct. 1461 (2018), the plurality held the unconstitutional exception severable, leaving the original exception-less robocall prohibition in place.

Much of the lack of a majority opinion was a function of the severability issue. GORSUCH, J., joined in part by Thomas, J., agreed with some of the plurality's analysis of the merits of the case but disagreed about severability. For Justice Gorsuch, the basic prohibition on robocalls to cell phones was itself an impermissible form of content regulation. As a result, he argued, severing the exception did not cure the basic problem, and he would have invalidated the entire prohibition. SOTOMAYOR, J., disagreed with the majority's content regulation analysis but concurred in the judgment because she agreed that the offending provision, if unconstitutional, was severable. BREYER, J., joined by Ginsburg and Kagan, JJ., reiterated his continuing concern with treating content regulation in almost all of its forms as triggering strict scrutiny. Although he consequently disagreed with the majority's view about the merits, he concurred in the judgment because he agreed that a provision that a majority of the Court had found constitutionally objectionable was severable from the entire statute.

CHAPTER 8

FREEDOM OF RELIGION

■ ■ ■

1. THE ESTABLISHMENT CLAUSE

IV. OFFICIAL ACKNOWLEDGMENT OF RELIGION

P. 1270, at end of note 1:

AMERICAN LEGION v. AMERICAN HUMANIST ASS'N, 139 S.Ct. 2067 (2019), again addressed the issue of public monuments with religious origins and connotations. At issue was the so-called Peace Cross in Bladensburg, Maryland. The cross was planned in 1918 as a memorial to the forty-nine Prince George's County solders who had been killed during the First World War. Finally constructed in 1925, the cross was a 32-foot tall "plain Latin cross" on a stone pedestal located on a traffic island at one end of one of the major highways connecting Washington, D.C., with Annapolis, Maryland. The cross, located on state-owned land and maintained by a state agency, was challenged as a violation of the Establishment Clause, but the Court, in a complex series of opinions, rejected the challenge, and in the process put what appears to be virtually the final nail in the coffin of the *Lemon* test.

ALITO, J., in an opinion that was mostly the opinion of the Court, noted that the *Lemon* test was especially unsuitable for "cases . . . that involve the use, for ceremonial, celebratory, or commemorative purposes, of words or symbols with religious associations," and that there should be a "presumption of constitutionality for longstanding monuments, symbols, and practices." More particularly, and as in *Salazar v. Buono*, infra, "[many] years after the fact . . . [there is] no way to be certain about the motivations of the men who were responsible for the creation of the monument." And as in *Van Orden*, supra, and *McCreary*, supra, "the purposes associated with an established monument, symbol, or practice often multiply." Moreover, "just as the purpose for maintaining a monument, symbol, or practice may evolve," so too may the message it conveys. And as a result, he said, the very act of removal may be understood as "aggressively hostile to removal."

Applying these concerns to the case at hand, Alito documented the way in which crosses in general, and not just this cross, had come to represent memorials to soldiers and to bravery. This was similar, he said, to the names of places, and "few would say that the State of California is attempting to convey a religious message by retaining the names given . . . by [the] original Spanish settlers [to] San Diego, Los Angeles, Santa Barbara, San Jose, San

Francisco, etc." "The cross is undoubtedly a Christian symbol, but that fact should not blind us to everything else that the Bladensburg Cross has come to represent. For some, that monument is a symbolic resting place for ancestors who never returned home. For others, it is a place for the community to gather and honor all veterans and their sacrifices for our Nation. For others still, it is a historical landmark. For many of these people, destroying [the] Cross that has stood undisturbed for nearly a century would not be neutral and would not further the ideals of respect and tolerance embodied in the First Amendment. [This] Cross does not offend the Constitution."

BREYER, J., joined by Kagan, J., concurred, observing that different considerations might apply to newer monuments in different contexts. KAVANAUGH, J, also concurred, explicitly emphasizing the way in which the *Lemon* test could not explain the Court's Establishment Clause jurisprudence for the 48 years since it was decided. But KAGAN, J., also concurring with most of Alito's opinion, remained of the belief that although "the *Lemon* test does not solve every Establishment Clause problem, [its] focus on purposes and effects [remains] crucial in evaluating government action in this sphere." THOMAS, J., concurring in the judgment, and describing the *Lemon* test as "long-discredited," reiterated his longstanding resistance to the incorporation of the Establishment Clause and thus its application to the states. "And even if [the Establishment Clause did apply to the states,] this religious display does not involve the type of actual legal coercion that was a hallmark of historical establishments of religion." GORSUCH, J., in an opinion joined by Thomas, J., concurred only in the judgment, insisting that merely being offended by the memorial's presence—"offended observer standing"—was insufficient to confer standing to sue in the first place, but also describing *Lemon* as a "misadventure." GINSBURG, J., joined by Sotomayor, J., dissented, documenting that most war memorials, including most of the World War I memorials, do not contain crosses or other religious symbols, and arguing that "[j]ust as a Star of David is not suitable to honor Christians who died serving their country, so is a cross not suitable to honor those of other faiths who died defending their nation. [By] maintaining the Peace Cross on a public highway, [Maryland] elevates Christianity over other faiths, and religion over nonreligion. [When] a cross is displayed on public property, the government may be presumed to endorse its religious content."

2. THE FREE EXERCISE CLAUSE AND RELATED STATUTORY ISSUES

I. CONFLICT WITH STATE REGULATION

P. 1305, at end of note 2:

Trinity Lutheran, in being about funding for the resurfacing of a religious school's playground, appeared to involve only state support for the non-religious activities of a religious institution. Whether the decision would also permit funding by a government program of general application for those parts of a religious institution that were more closely related to the institution's religious mission remained an open question. That question became less open, however, after the Court's 2020 decision in ESPINOZA v. MONTANA DEPARTMENT OF REVENUE, 140 S.Ct. ___, 2020 WL 3518364 (2020).

At issue in *Espinoza* was a Montana program providing a $150 tax credit to those who made donations to organizations awarding scholarships for private school tuition. Under the Montana program, the tax credit was available without regard to whether the private schools that were supported (by the choice of the scholarship recipients) were religious or secular. Although a program allowing such indirect support for religious schools would not, under existing doctrine, run afoul of the Establishment Clause (*Locke*; *Trinity Lutheran*), both the Montana Department of Revenue and then the Montana Supreme Court concluded that the program nevertheless violated the "no aid" provision of the Montana Constitution, a provision prohibiting "direct or indirect" public funding of any school, college, or university "controlled in whole or in part by any church, sect, or denomination." The issue before the Court in *Espinoza* was whether excluding religious schools from benefiting from an indirect funding program of general application, as the Montana Supreme Court concluded that the Montana Constitution required, violated the Free Exercise Clause of the First Amendment.

Writing for a 5–4 majority, ROBERTS, C.J., held that Montana's exclusion of schools operated by religious organizations from an otherwise comprehensive program of support for private schools violated the Free Exercise Clause. Relying heavily on *Trinity Lutheran*, the majority concluded that "disqualifying otherwise eligible recipients from a public benefit 'solely because of their religious character' triggered strict Free Exercise scrutiny, and that Montana had not demonstrated that the exclusion served interests "of the highest order" (*Lukumi*) and was "narrowly tailored in pursuit of those interests."

Unlike *Locke*, which involved support for the training of clergy, there was no indication in *Espinoza* that the indirect funding would necessarily wind up supporting explicitly religious activities. But the Court found such a distinction unavailing, and indeed irrelevant, concluding that strict Free Exercise scrutiny was triggered by discrimination based on the religious *status* of an institution, without regard to whether the supported activities—the *use* of the funds—were or were not religious in character.

THOMAS, J., joined by Gorsuch, J., concurred with the majority opinion, but wrote separately to reiterate his view that the Fourteenth Amendment did not incorporate the Establishment Clause. For Justice Thomas, the Establishment Clause was too-often employed to validate what would otherwise be Free Exercise violations, and "unincorporating" the Establishment Clause would remove a frequent obstacle to full realization of Free Exercise values.

ALITO, J., also issued a concurring opinion, detailing the way in which Montana's "no aid" constitutional provision, like those in thirty-eight other states, was modeled after the ultimately unsuccessful attempts in the "Blaine Amendment" proposal of 1876 to amend the United States Constitution. The Blaine Amendment movement, Justice Alito argued, was based on explicitly anti-Catholic sentiments, sentiments arising out of anti-immigrant feelings that were pervasive at the time. This history, Justice Alito suggested, provided the context in which Montana's actions should be viewed, a context highlighting the anti-religious motivations that should even now inform the understanding of "sectarian" in provisions such as that in the Montana Constitution. And GORSUCH, J.,'s separate concurring opinion focused on the status/use distinction, arguing that "[t]he right to *be* religious without the right to *do* religious things would hardly amount to a right at all."

GINSBURG, J., joined by Kagan, J., dissented, emphasizing the fact that the Montana Supreme Court had, because it believed that the scholarship program violated the Montana Constitution's no-aid provision, invalidated the entire program. For Justice Ginsburg, this meant that there was no program in place, thus eliminating any possibility of discrimination between secular and sectarian schools. Under the Montana Supreme Court's ruling, she insisted, no one received anything, and thus there could be no claim that secular institutions were receiving benefits or support that sectarian institutions were not. [In his majority opinion, Chief Justice Roberts addressed this argument, maintaining that the Montana Supreme Court's invalidation of the entire program was based on a misreading of *federal* constitutional law, a misreading that the Supreme Court was empowered to correct.]

BREYER, J, also dissented, joined in part by Kagan, J. He objected to an "overly rigid" application of the combination of the Establishment and Free Exercise Clauses, urging the majority to be faithful to the "play-in-the-joints" idea suggested in *Trinity Lutheran*. Applying this more flexible and context-specific approach, Breyer took issue with the majority's focus on the status of the recipient institutions and argued that what should matter was what the institution would *do* with the support. And he saw the Montana situation as one in which the recipient institutions, as in *Locke*, would be using state support "for the inculcation of religious truths" precisely because "religious schools seek generally to inspire religious faith and values in their students."

SOTOMAYOR, J., dissented as well, agreeing with Justice Ginsburg that, with no program in force, there was no extant discrimination and thus no case to decide. And Justice Sotomayor also reprised her dissent in *Trinity Lutheran*, seeing the Montana Supreme Court's decision as amounting to little more than a refusal by the state to "pay for [a] religious practice," a refusal that did not violate the Free Exercise Clause.

CHAPTER 9

EQUAL PROTECTION

■ ■ ■

2. RACE AND ETHNIC ANCESTRY

IV. DE JURE VS. DE FACTO DISCRIMINATION

P. 1454, after *Abbott v. Perez*:

———

In DEPARTMENT OF HOMELAND SECURITY v. REGENTS OF UNIVERSITY OF CALIFORNIA, 140 S.Ct. 1891 (2020), the Court, per ROBERTS, C.J., held that the Department of Homeland Security violated the Administrative Procedure Act (by failing to provide an adequately reasoned explanation for its decision) when it rescinded an order allowing unauthorized aliens who arrived in the United States as children to apply for temporary suspension of removal. At the same time, the Court held that the challengers had not adequately pleaded a claim that the agency acted for racially discriminatory reasons. The plaintiffs had cited no evidence of discriminatory motive by the immediately responsible officials—the Attorney General and the Acting Secretary of the Department of Homeland Security—and statements by President Trump that allegedly manifest hostility to Latinos were "remote in time and made in unrelated contexts." Sotomayor, J., dissented on the equal protection question: "[T]he impact of the policy decision must be viewed in the context of the President's public statements on and off the campaign trail."

4. SPECIAL SCRUTINY FOR OTHER CLASSIFICATIONS: DOCTRINE AND DEBATES

I. SEXUAL ORIENTATION

P. 1545, at the end of note 3:

In *Bostock v. Clayton County*, 140 S.Ct. 1731 (2020), the Court, per Gorsuch, J., held by 6–3 that an employer's firing of an employee "simply for being homosexual or transgender" constitutes forbidden discrimination on the basis of "sex" under Title VII of the 1964 Civil Rights Act: "Consider, for example, an employer with two employees, both of whom are attracted to men. The two individuals are, to the employer's mind, materially identical in all respects, except that one is a man and the other a woman. If the employer fires the male employee for no reason other than the fact he is attracted to men, the employer discriminates against him for traits or actions it tolerates in his female colleague . . . . It doesn't matter if other factors besides the plaintiff's sex contributed to the decision."

Alito, J., joined by Thomas, J., dissented, as did Kavanaugh, J. The dissenting opinions stressed that "sex discrimination" and discrimination based on LGBT status are different concepts that reflect different attitudes and motivations. Alito, J., thought it among *Bostock*'s likely consequences that "despite the important differences between the Fourteenth Amendment and Title VII, the Court's decision may exert a gravitational pull" toward subjecting anti-LGBT discrimination to the same elevated scrutiny as sex discrimination in suits alleging constitutional violations.

5. FUNDAMENTAL RIGHTS

I. VOTING

D. "Dilution" of the Right: Partisan Gerrymanders

P. 1608, after the first full paragraph, substitute the following paragraph for *Davis v. Bandemer*, *Vieth v. Jubelirer*, and the Notes and Questions that follow on pages 1616–19:

In DAVIS v. BANDEMER, 478 U.S. 109 (1986), the Court divided over the test to apply to identify constitutionally forbidden partisan gerrymanders under the Equal Protection Clause. WHITE, J., joined by Brennan, Marshall, and Blackmun, JJ., would have required proof of "intentional discrimination against an identifiable political group and an actual discriminatory effect on that group." POWELL, J., joined by Stevens, J., would have focused on "whether the boundaries of the voting districts have been distorted deliberately and arbitrarily to achieve illegitimate ends." A dissenting opinion, by O'CONNOR, J., joined by Burger, C.J., and Rehnquist, J., would have held that challenges to partisan gerrymanders pose nonjusticiable political questions because the Equal Protection Clause simply "does not supply judicially manageable standards for resolving" them.

The view that challenges to partisan gerrymanders present political questions, which gained the support of a plurality of the Justices in *Vieth v. Jubelier*, 541 U.S. 267 (2004), prevailed, by a vote of 5 to 4, in *Rucho v. Common Cause*, p. 1 of this Supplement. *Rucho*, which you should re-read at this time, states the governing law on the constitutional permissibility of partisan gerrymanders. As you re-read Roberts, C.J.'s, majority opinion, consider what practical difference there is, if any, between its ruling that challengers to political gerrymanders pose nonjusticiable political questions and an "on the merits" conclusion that partisan gerrymanders do not violate the Equal Protection Clause or any other provision of the Constitution.

CHAPTER 10

THE CONCEPT OF STATE ACTION

■ ■ ■

2. "GOVERNMENT FUNCTION"

III. REFUSALS TO FIND "GOVERNMENTAL FUNCTION"

P. 1674, after *Jackson v. Metropolitan Edison Co.*:

———

MANHATTAN COMMUNITY ACCESS CORP. v. HALLECK, 139 S.Ct. 1921 (2019), held that a private entity administering the public access channels on a New York cable system was not a state actor despite having been designated to perform that function by the City of New York. New York state law "requires cable operators in the State to set aside channels on their cable systems for public access" and further "requires that use of the public access channels be free of charge and first-come, first-served. Under state law, the cable operator operates the public access channels unless the local government in the area chooses to itself operate the channels or designates a private entity to operate the channels." For the Time-Warner cable system in Manhattan, New York City designated a private nonprofit corporation, Manhattan Neighborhood Network (MNN), to operate the legally mandated public access channels. After the respondents produced a film critical of MNN and MNN televised it, MNN suspended the respondents from further access to MNN facilities. Respondents then sued, alleging that the public access channels were a public forum and that MNN's actions violated their First Amendment rights.

Per KAVANAUGH, J., the Court, by 5–4, ordered dismissal on the ground that MNN is not a state actor. Although "a private entity may qualify as a state actor when it exercises 'powers traditionally exclusively reserved to the State,'" *Jackson v. Metropolitan Edison Co.*, the function of operating "public access channels on a cable system [h]as not traditionally and exclusively been performed by government. Since the 1970s, when public access channels became a regular feature on cable systems, a variety of private and public actors have operated public access channels, including: private cable operators; private nonprofit organizations;

43

municipalities; and other public and private community organizations such as churches, schools, and libraries." As the Court ruled in *Hudgens* v. *NLRB*, "a private entity who provides a forum for speech is not transformed by that fact alone into a state actor. [G]rocery stores put up community bulletin boards. Comedy clubs host open mic nights."

Nor did it matter that New York City had "designated MNN to operate the public access channels" or that "New York State heavily regulates MNN with respect to the public access channels. [That] the government licenses, contracts with, or grants a monopoly to a private entity does not convert the private entity into a state actor—unless the private entity is performing a traditional, exclusive public function."

Kavanaugh, J., dismissed an alternative contention that MNN was a state actor because it acted in the stead of New York City, which should be regarded as the owner or lessor of the public access channels under applicable New York law. "It does not matter that a provision in the franchise agreements between the City and Time Warner allowed the City to designate a private entity to operate the public access channels on Time Warner's cable system. [N]othing in the franchise agreements suggests that the City possesses any property interest in Time Warner's cable system, or in the public access channels on that system."

SOTOMAYOR, J., dissented: "New York City secured a property interest in public-access television channels when it granted a cable franchise to a cable company. State regulations require those public-access channels to be made open to the public on terms that render them a public forum. The City contracted out the administration of that forum to a private organization. [By] accepting that agency relationship, MNN stepped into the City's shoes and thus qualifies as a state actor.

"[The majority] is wrong in two ways. First, the majority erroneously decides the property question against the plaintiffs as a matter of law. [S]econd, and more fundamentally, the majority mistakes a case about the government choosing to hand off responsibility to an agent for a case about a private entity that simply enters a marketplace. [The] majority's opinion erroneously fixates on a type of case that is not before us: one [such as *Jackson*] in which a private entity simply enters the marketplace and is then subject to government regulation. [But] MNN is not a private entity that simply ventured into the marketplace. It occupies its role because it was asked to do so by the City, which secured the public-access channels in exchange for giving up public rights of way, opened those channels up (as required by the State) as a public forum, and then deputized MNN to administer them." The Court's reliance on prior public function cases was therefore misguided. "[When] the government hires an agent, [that agent is a state actor, regardless of whether the government] hired the agent to do something that can be done in the private marketplace too."

CHAPTER 12

LIMITATIONS ON JUDICIAL POWER AND REVIEW

■ ■ ■

2. STANDING

I. THE STRUCTURE OF STANDING DOCTRINE

P. 1757, after the second paragraph of note 9:

In *June Medical Services LLC. v. Russo*, 140 S.Ct. ___, 2020 WL 3492640 (2020), p. 22, supra, a divided Court allowed abortion doctors to assert the rights of their patients in challenging a statute that required any doctor who performs abortions to have admitting privileges at a nearby hospital. Dissenting, Alito, J., joined by Thomas and Gorsuch, JJ., argued that conflict-of-interest principles should bar the doctors' assertion of women's rights to challenge a statute ostensibly enacted to protect women's health.

II. CONGRESSIONAL POWER TO CREATE STANDING

P. 1766, at the end of note 2:

Thole v. U.S. Bank N.A., 140 S.Ct. 1615 (2020), held that retired participants in the Bank's defined-benefit retirement plan lacked standing to challenge alleged mismanagement of the plan, despite a provision of the Employee Retirement Income Security Act (ERISA) authorizing suits by plan beneficiaries. Because the plaintiffs had been paid all benefits due in the past, and were "legally and contractually entitled to receive . . . [fixed] monthly payments for the rest of their lives," the Court found that they had suffered no cognizable injury.

Sotomayor, J., joined by Ginsburg, Breyer, and Kagan, JJ., dissented. "Because ERISA requires that retirement-plan assets be held in trust," beneficiaries had "equitable interests" in "their retirement plan's financial integrity"—analogous to those recognized by the traditional law of trusts—that had incurred injuries. Sotomayor, J., also argued that the statutory authorization to sue effectively empowered beneficiaries to sue on behalf of the plan, which clearly would have had standing to protect its own assets. By contrast, the Court emphasized that there had been no formal assignment of plan's interests to the beneficiaries.

3. TIMING OF ADJUDICATION

I. MOOTNESS

P. 1780, at the end of note 3:

In *New York State Rifle & Pistol Ass'n, Inc. v. City of New York*, 140 S.Ct. 1525 (2020), the Court ruled that a challenge to a New York City ordinance that barred licensed gun owners from transporting their weapons anywhere besides seven firing ranges within the City became moot after New York adopted an amended ordinance that allowed "direct[ ]" transport to and from other gun ranges and second homes. Dissenting, Alito, J., joined by Thomas and Gorsuch, JJ., maintained that because the amended ordinance continued to burden the petitioners' asserted right of "unrestricted access" to gun ranges, the dispute remained live.